# Christmas
# *Quilling*

# EM
## Elizabeth Moad

www.elizabethmoad.com

First Published in 2010

ISBN 978-0-9566209-0-3

Printed in Mexico
Editor: Jo Richardson
Designer: Sarah Wade
Photographer: Karl Adamson

# CONTENTS

# INTRODUCTION

It has been a real pleasure for me working on the quilled projects for this book, developing the ideas from concept to reality. Handmade cards are an essential part of the festive season for me, affording the chance to display new techniques learned during the year, changes in style and developments in creativity, as well as to share news and send greetings to friends and family. A handcrafted Christmas card is also sure to be treasured by whoever receives it, as they will recognize that so much more thought and care has been put into creating it than selecting and writing a shop-bought card. In this age of mass production and uniformity, a quilled card will stand out a long way from commercial designs.

The historic craft of quilling comes into its own at Christmas time, the intricacies of the technique offering a variety of intriguing effects. In this source book I have assembled a wide range of quilling card projects for you to dip into while preparing for the holiday season, and each design is presented with a step-by-step guide to the particular techniques involved, to ensure successful results. Here, quilling is used to make traditional motifs such as holly and bells, but it is also given a modern twist using vibrant tones and bold compositions to bring it bang up to date, with inspiration drawn from the contemporary colour schemes and cutting-edge design ideas that pop up each year.

Although there is a wealth of ideas for you to choose from in this book, don't be afraid to adapt a design to suit your personal colour preferences or those of the recipient.

I am delighted to share these unique festive card designs with you so that your quilling is successful and gratifying, both to make and to receive.

## A Potted History of Quilling

Paper quilling, or paper filigree as it is sometimes called, has its roots in history around 500 years ago. The exact origins are not known, as paper degrades over time, but it is thought that the first quillers were among members of religious households who created paper art for devotional purposes. Examples dating back to Georgian and Victorian times do still exist, when decorating tea caddies and boxes with rolled paper shapes was regarded as an appropriate leisure pursuit for ladies. The papers were rolled around the quills of bird feathers, and this was how the craft gained its name. Quilling became popular in England in the late 18th and early 19th centuries and from here it spread to the American colonies. Quilling subsequently suffered a decline, but it has since resurfaced to become a popular 21st-century craft that is practised throughout the world.

## Quilling on the Run

The projects in this book vary in the time and effort they take to make. Some are more complex cards, such as Poinsettia Posy, pages 24–25, while others are quicker, for example Swirly Trees, pages 48–49. There are those crafters who are ultra organized and start making their cards way before the Christmas season, but the majority – myself included! – find that time has just slipped away. This doesn't mean that you have to abandon all hope of completing your special handcrafted cards, as quilling can easily be done on the run.

Take with you wherever you go, travelling on a train or bus or even round at a neighbouring crafter's home while having a coffee, a small plastic box with your basic quilling essentials: quilling tool, glue and cocktail stick (toothpick) scissors and the papers for the project. You can then seize any opportunity or spare time to make coiled and pinched shapes in order to build up a stock ready to assemble when you are back at your craft desk. It's surprising just how much you can achieve by putting these few moments in the day to productive use.

## Practical Tips

* Stock up on quilling papers, blank cards and embellishments.
* Always use good-quality card blanks, as the cards need to stand up for a long time, and cheaper, thin cards will buckle and look unsightly.
* Choose simpler designs for mass production – to save time, you can reduce a more complex design to a minimalist-style card.
* Work in good light to avoid straining your eyes, and don't spend long periods of time quilling without taking a break.
* Make sure the quilled design is glued on well so that the coils don't fall off in the post.
* Take extra care when adding greetings to cards – this is often the final part to be completed and a design can be ruined if it's rushed.
* Make matching tags for gifts by taking an element from the main card design.
* Plan postage and buy ready-made posting boxes.
* And don't panic if in the countdown to Christmas you run out of time – there's always next year!

# Papers

As eggs are to an omelette, paper is the one single, key ingredient for quilling, and the foundation of the whole technique. It's possible to cut your own strips of paper, but most quillers purchase pre-cut strips to the width they require in the colours they want. Pre-cut strips not only save time but they are exactly uniform in width. Many suppliers will trim paper to the width you require, but wider strips will tend to cost slightly more. Quilling is not an expensive hobby, so do indulge in some extra-special papers for your festive cards.

## Colour

Christmas is an event that allows you to use any colour, so don't be restricted to the traditional reds and greens. Explore further by using bright pinks or more subtle ivory or white. Metallic-edged papers are very popular, as they shimmer and glint in the light – ideal for quilled shapes.

## Weights

The weight of paper used for quilling is critical and this is why it's best to purchase strips rather than cut your own. The paper should be around 100gsm in weight, which is strong enough to coil easily and hold its shape. Paper of a lighter weight isn't easy to work with because it's too flimsy, and conversely paper that's relatively heavy or thick is too stiff to coil.

## Widths

Pre-cut paper strips come in several standard widths, as personal preference varies with the crafter, and the choice of width will also depend on what is being made. The following widths of paper are used this book:

1.5–2mm (1/16in) – the minimum width that's available
3mm (1/8in) – this is the most common width and ideal for beginners
5mm (3/16in) – this width is good for more definition
10mm (3/8in) – this is the most common width for use with a fringing tool

## Storage

If you are a beginner to quilling, once you have accumulated your quilling papers it's important to store them so that they are easily accessible and won't become tangled. Plastic storage units are readily available and inexpensive, allowing you to organize the papers according to colour, width and special finishes.

# QUILLING TOOLS

I have always used a quilling tool – the one pictured here – and teach classes using a tool because I find it easy to use and to achieve quick results. A quilling tool has a two-pronged slot through which to thread paper, and the handle makes it easy to turn for coiling. However, not all quillers use a tool to make coils, as some prefer to make them by rolling the paper around a needle tool or just using their fingers. The advantage of a quilling tool is that the slot catches the end of the paper, whereas the needle tool requires the paper to be wrapped around it. The disadvantage of the quilling tool is that it leaves a kink in the centre of the coil, which coiling around a needle tool does not. There are times when I don't want this kink, and in those cases I use a needle tool or a needle in a cork, so a combination of both methods is a practical approach. But it is of course a matter of personal preference and I never prescribe what to use – as long as people are quilling, I'm happy!

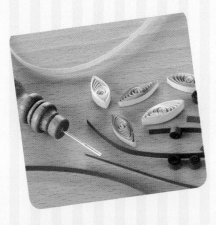

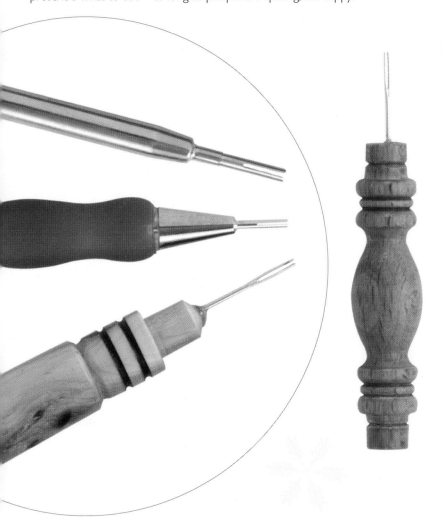

My quilling tool is used throughout this book, as pictured left and above from Gilded Garlands, pages 52–53. It has travelled far and wide with me across the world, and miraculously I haven't managed to lose it!

The wooden quilling tool pictured left in its entirety has a very narrow slot, just wide enough to fit the paper through, thus creating a very small centre in a tight coil. This is demonstrated in Poinsettia Posy (see above), pages 24–25, and Ding-dong Merrily (see below), pages 36–37.

Quilling tools come in all shapes and sizes, but are all essentially the same design with a slot for the paper and a handle. Quilling tools can be very cheap to purchase, but even the most expensive is not a lot of money and they last a lifetime with care. I have used the same tool for 10 years. It is, however, important to find the tool that suits you. Some people prefer long handles, while others favour shorter handles that fit into the palm of the hand. When choosing a quilling tool, look at the size of the gap at the curling end: a larger gap in the tool means a large gap in the centre of the coil and this is most noticeable when making tight coils.

# QUILLING KIT

The following is a guide to the basic essentials needed for quilling. This is not an exhaustive list and more experienced crafters may use other tools and embellishing materials.

## BASIC TOOLS

### Cutting mat, craft knife and metal ruler
A self-healing cutting mat is essential when cutting with a craft knife and metal ruler, and also protects your work surface.

### Fine-tipped tweezers
These are used for picking up, pinching and positioning coils, gemstones and so on. The pair shown is self-locking so that you don't need to keep them squeezed.

### PVA (white) glue
It's best to use a tacky PVA (white) glue, as it dries quickly and is not too runny. Apply the glue with a cocktail stick (toothpick).

### Large circle punch or shape cutter and template
You should use one or other of these tools for cutting large circles from card, such as a circle aperture in a card blank, to achieve a professional finish.

### Needle tool
This is a metal point on a handle, useful for rolling paper around and leaving a hole in the centre. Some quillers like to use a needle tool for applying a dot of glue instead of using a cocktail stick (toothpick).

### Small, fine-pointed scissors
These are essential for snipping and trimming papers.

### HB pencil and eraser
These items are required for marking lines on graph paper and for tracing templates.

### Quilling board
This template board is cork- or foam-based with a plastic top that has cut-out circles of various sizes. The cork or foam is recessed, allowing you to insert a coil and let it unwind while constrained by the plastic edges. A quilling board enables you to create exactly the same size of coil every time.

### Fringing tool
These tools are so called because they 'fringe' paper. By manually moving the handle of the tool up and down, the paper is sliced at a 90-degree angle. However, it doesn't cut right across the paper but leaves an uncut margin so that the paper stays in one piece. As you move the handle up and down, the paper is pulled through, enabling you to fringe a whole length in no time at all.

### Board and pins
Used for the husking technique (see pages 30–31), a thick piece of foam, polystyrene or Styrofoam board allows pins to be inserted in order to position and hold papers in place.

# EMBELLISHING TOOLS AND MATERIALS

Quilled designs can be decorated or enhanced with a few extra items, and here is a representative selection of the additional tools and materials used in the book.

### Small circle punches

Differing sizes of small circle punch are useful for making holes to contain quilling shapes (see Funky Tree, pages 26–27), but also for making holes for ribbon in cards.

### Glitter glue

Easier to apply than traditional dry glitter, this glue allows more precise application using the handy nozzle.

### Scallop-edged scissors

These scissors are a useful toolbox addition, used to cut card in Pear Tree, pages 22–23, and the decorative paper for Clean and Contemporary, page 25, pictured below.

### 3D paint

This paint has more volume than ordinary paint, so it's used for adding colour to flower centres (see Poinsettia Posy, pages 24–25).

### Swarovski crystals

These are specialist stones with a point, so they are set into quilled shapes (see Crystal Snowflake, pages 32–33), but they reflect more light than ordinary flat-backed gemstones.

# Basic Techniques

In quilling, the end result is determined by the length of paper used, how much the coil is allowed to unwind and if the end of the coiled paper is glued in place. These three factors are explored and demonstrated here.

## How to Make a Coil

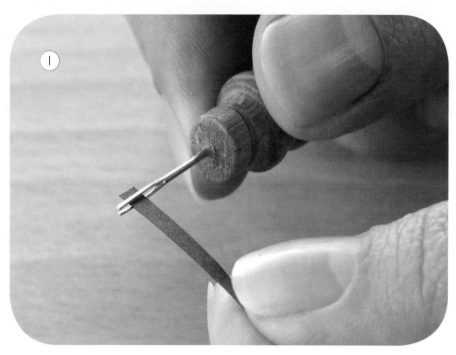

Insert a strip of paper into the slot of the quilling tool 2mm (1/16in) from the end of the paper. If you are a beginner, it's best to use 3mm (1/8in) wide paper, which is the width used in these examples.

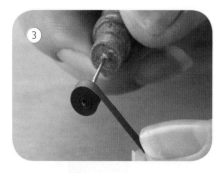

Turn the quilling tool to catch the end of the paper strip. Continue to turn the tool. I always turn the tool away from me, as I find this gives me most control, but there is no hard and fast rule. Guide the coil with your fingers and keep a light tension on the paper with your spare hand.

Continue turning the quilling tool until the end of the paper is reached, then carefully remove the tool by sliding the paper off the prongs, holding the coiled paper in place.

Release the coil a little and then glue the end of the strip to the coil to create a loose closed coil.

Alternatively, without releasing the coil, add a dot of glue to the end of the strip with a cocktail stick (toothpick) and press to the coil to make a tight coil.

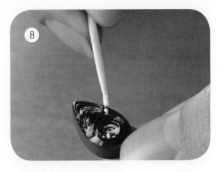

If you release the coil further, the coil will become larger in diameter.

Release the coil even further or let go altogether to create an open coil.

Apply a small amount of PVA (white) glue over one side of the coil, making sure that the centre and outer edges have glue on.

Alternatively, insert the coil into a template in a quilling board to achieve a specific size of coil. A quilling board is used in Simply Stockings, pages 38–39, to make the coils for the hearts identical, and in Present Perfect, pages 46–47, for creating even-sized coils for the bows.

For this Berry Wreath design on page 44, tight coils are made following Steps 1–4 opposite, and then the centres pushed into dome shapes.

# Loose Closed Coils

These are shapes that are created where the end of the paper has been glued to the coil. Here, the initial coil has been allowed to unwind a little and become loose, but the coil is closed.

**Teardrop** Pinch one end to a point.

**Bent teardrop** Pinch one end and then pull this point round at an angle.

**Off-centre teardrop** Pull the centre of the coil to one side and make sure that the inner coils are evenly spaced, then pinch on that side.

**Eye** (sometimes called a marquise) Pinch at two opposing points.

**Triangle** Pinch at three points an equal distance apart.

# Loose Closed Coil Shapes

**Square** Pinch at two points as for the eye and then pinch at another equally spaced two points.

**Diamond** Pinch as for the square, but squeeze gently at two points.

**Crescent** Pinch at two opposing points, then pull the pinched points round and inwards to bend.

Bent teardrop shapes are used to create the mistletoe for this Christmas Kiss card design on page 19.

If you're a novice quiller, make as many shapes as possible to practise, and don't worry if a few go wrong!

# Loose Closed Coils

**Star** Pinch at four equally spaced points and then press inwards towards the centre.

**Rectangle** Pinch at two opposing points, then pinch again at two opposing points a short distance from the first two pinched points.

**Holly leaf** Instructions for making holly leaf shapes are given on page 40. The series of pinches involved are assisted by using tweezers to achieve the pointed edges.

**Half circle** Pinch at two points relatively close together, leaving the curve of the coil intact on the opposite side of the coil.

**Heart** Pinch into a teardrop, hold the point in one hand and simultaneously push inwards with a fingernail at the opposing point.

I find that beginners are hesitant and gentle, when you can actually be quite tough in pinching, pulling and squeezing the coils.

Holly leaf shapes are used to make this Holly Spray design on page 40 and as an accent for the Merry Message card on page 34.

# OPEN COILS

For open coils, the paper is coiled with the quilling tool, then the tool removed and the coil left to find its own shape without being glued at all. As the end of the paper strip is not glued and is left 'open', this is why they are known as open coils.

The variety of these open coils is endless because the length of paper can be folded at differing points and the ends coiled. Two lengths that have been made into open coils can then be glued together or a pinched coil can be glued to an open coil (see Scrolled Noel, pages 50–51).

A needle tool is used to roll paper around for an open coil in Pretty Patterns, pages 20–21, the preferred tool in this instance to avoid the kink that a quilling tool leaves.

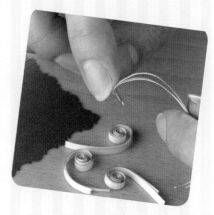

For a different effect, fold a length of paper in half and then coil around a needle tool for a double-thickness open coil, as featured in Dove of Peace, pages 28–29.

Open coils are used for the tail of the Diminutive Dove on page 28 to give a lighter effect and to complement the pinched closed coils of the dove's body and wings.

If you don't have a needle tool, make your own by setting a fine sewing needle into a dense wine cork.

# PROJECTS

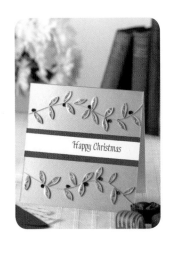

# Mistlestoe Wishes

Sprigs of mistletoe are a favourite festive trimming in houses at Christmastime mainly due to the age-old tradition of kissing under them! For the paper version of mistletoe, quilled teardrop shapes are bent and held in place while the glue dries to create the characteristic curved shape of the leaves. The convincing-looking white berries are tight closed coils formed into dome shapes. Finished off with a tie of delicate organza ribbon, this delightful card is ideal for a loved one at Christmas or an anniversary card.

*You will need....*

- papers: 3mm (1/8in) wide green, white
- light green card and matching card blank
- green organza ribbon 1cm (3/8in) wide

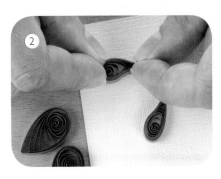

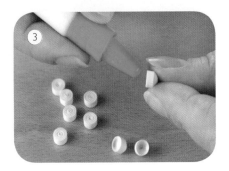

1 For the mistletoe leaves, use a quilling tool to make a loose closed coil from a 40cm (15 3/4in) length of the green paper. Pull the centre of the coil to one side using one hand, and with the other hand pinch the shape to a point and pull the point round at an angle to make a bent teardrop shape. Make nine more.

2 Apply glue all over one side of the bent teardrop shape and place on the light green card. To maintain the curved leaf shape, hold the quilled teardrop in place while the glue dries, which generally takes about five seconds, but the exact time will depend on the tackiness of the glue you are using.

3 For the mistletoe berries, use the quilling tool to make tight coils from seven 20cm (8in) lengths of the white paper, gluing the end in place. Use the tip of your little finger or a lid to push up the centre of the coil to make a dome shape – the nozzle of a tube of glue is the ideal size here. Place a generous amount of glue inside each dome shape and leave to dry.

SENTIMENT SUGGESTIONS

Give the Gift of Love this Christmastime

Spread Christmas Cheer this Season

Holiday Hugs and Kisses to You

A Christmas Kiss Just for You

## Mistletoe Garland

Here, four sprigs of mistletoe are glued onto a strip of light green card and the stems glued together at the top. Green organza ribbon 5cm (2in) wide is wrapped around a green card blank and the green card mounted so that it overlaps the ribbon. A smaller sprig of mistletoe is made by using two 20cm (8in) lengths of 3mm (1/8in) wide green paper and a 10cm (4in) length of 3mm (1/8in) wide white paper. A mini tag is punched from the same light green card, then threaded with 1cm (3/8in) wide light green organza ribbon and tied around the card.

Tip . . .

Silver glitter glue could
be added to the tops
of the mistletoe berries
as in the Berry Merry
card, pages 44–45.

# Finishing the Card

Glue the leaves onto the light green card in pairs with 10cm (4in) lengths of
the green paper in between the leaves for the stems, to form five sprigs. Then
glue the stems together near to the top of each length. Trim off the excess
paper and tie green organza ribbon around the stems in a bow. Glue on the
white berries so that they are snug inside the leaves. Glue the light green card
panel to a matching card blank. Add a message or Christmas greeting if you
wish, such as 'Sending you love and kisses at Christmas'.

# Christmas Kiss

For this card, the mistletoe sprigs hang free, framed within a heart aperture.
The leaves are made as in Step 1 of the main card, but glued to acetate
instead of card. When the glue is dry, the leaves are easily removed from the
acetate and glued together with a stem, with white berries, made as before,
glued to the leaves. Three of the stems are then glued together. Two holes
are punched in the red aperture card blank at the top of the heart and light
green organza ribbon threaded through, then tied around the stems. A square
of green card is attached to the inside of the back panel of the red card.

# Pretty Patterns

A bauble hanging within an aperture is decorated for a bold, contemporary effect by using a single shade of red paper against a simple white background. The quilled patterning is created with a combination of open coils and pinched shapes, intricately laid out to form a repeating pattern that can cover as large an area as you wish. The density of the coils can be altered, as shown in the variation cards.

## You will need....

- paper: 2mm (1/16in) wide red
- white card
- light blue square card blank
- thin wire
- blue fibre thread
- large circle punch or shape cutter and template
- adhesive tape

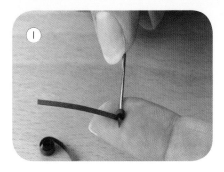

1 Cut a circle of white card, which will need to be smaller than your proposed aperture in the card blank (see template on page 59). To make the open coils, using a needle tool and a 5cm (2in) length of the red paper, start by rolling the end of the paper tightly around the tool and then use one hand to turn the tool and the other to guide the paper. Stop coiling just before the end of the paper is reached. Glue one coil to the white card circle near the edge, applying glue under the coil.

2 Using a quilling tool, make loose closed coils from 10cm (4in) lengths of the red paper and pinch at either end into leaf shapes. Glue one leaf shape next to the open coil glued onto the white card circle. Apply a dot of glue at the end of the open coil and position the next open coil so that it touches the glue. You will also need to put glue under this coil.

3 Continue to build up the pattern using the open coils and pinched leaf shapes. It's best to try not to be too rigid when creating the pattern and just let it evolve as you go along, but with a check now and again that you are achieving the effect you desire.

## Tip . . .

This design suits larger motifs, such as the tree, bauble and stocking here. Other appropriate ones are a star, wreath or gift.

## Textured Tree

The tree shape is cut from white card, using the template on page 58, and then decorated with the same arrangement of open and pinched coils as for the main card. However, here the coils and leaves are packed closely together, leaving little white space between them for a denser look to the pattern, which will require more paper, more coils and, yes, more time! But it depends on the look you want for your finished card. Ribbon is tied through a notch in the spine of a blue card blank, which has a darker blue panel added to the lower part, and tied at one side. The tree is then mounted over the top with foam pads.

Tip . . .
Here 2mm (1/16in) wide paper is used, but you could use 3mm (1/8in) wide paper instead. Be prepared – a needle tool isn't as easy as a quilling tool to use, as the latter catches the paper.

# FINISHING THE CARD

Cut a circle aperture in a light blue square card blank, ensuring that the aperture is slightly bigger than the bauble – remember to use a large circle punch or a shape cutter and template to achieve a professional finish. Cut a top for the bauble from white card and attach a small loop of wire, then attach blue fibre thread with adhesive tape. Wrap the fibre thread around the top of the card and tie in a knot so that the bauble hangs free. The bauble would look equally good mounted directly onto a card with a greeting as an alternative to the aperture.

# SQUIGGLE STOCKING

This cute dangling stocking is again decorated with open coils and leaf shapes, but the pattern is less dense than for the main card, and by spacing out the coils and leaves, a larger surface area can be covered more quickly. A stocking is cut from white card and the top, toe and heal from red card – template on page 60. The latter are attached to the white stocking and a loop of narrow blue ribbon added to the top. The stocking is then mounted onto blue card and then a different-toned blue card blank with a mini wooden peg at the top.

# Pear Tree

This stylish tree dripping with golden pears recalls those well-loved words from the traditional Christmas carol 'a partridge in a pear tree'. The tree is set against a red background to contrast with the gold-edged quilled coils, and this in turn is mounted onto green patterned paper for an added highlight. The tree trunk and pot are cut from gold card, then lavishly wrapped with organza ribbon. As well as making a sumptuous Christmas card, this design could be used either as a special invitation or a 'thank you' card.

## You will need....

- papers: 3mm (1/8in) wide green, gold-edged ivory
- card: red, gold
- green patterned paper
- green card blank
- green organza ribbon 3mm (1/8in) wide
- scallop-edged scissors

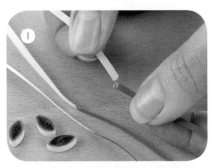

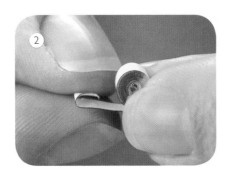

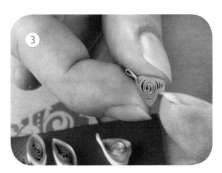

1 Attach a 15cm (6in) length of the green paper to a 10cm (4in) length of the gold-edged ivory paper. Starting from the green paper, use a quilling tool to coil right to the end of the ivory paper. Make a loose closed coil and pinch both ends to create a leaf shape. Repeat to make 16 leaves in total. Then make 27 plain green leaves from 15cm (6in) lengths of the green paper in the same way.

2 For the pears, make a coil with a 20cm (8in) length of gold-edged ivory paper using the quilling tool. Remove the tool and place glue 1cm (3/8in) from the end of the paper. Fold over the end of the paper and press the tip of the paper against the glue to make a tiny loop.

3 Let the coil release a little and then gently pinch the top near the loop so that it presses into the glue. Continue holding the top of the shape and with a fingernail push the bottom of the shape inwards, making an indent. Repeat to make five pears in total.

## Bountiful Branches

For this variation, branches laden with pears and leaves grow either side of a main stem. Only leaves made with the green and gold-edged ivory papers, not plain green leaves, are used for this card. First, glue three leaves at the top of a green card square with a stem of paper hanging downwards. Then position lengths of green paper either side for the branches and glue six pears in place. Glue the remaining leaves in position and the branches to the leaves and pears (see Gilded Garlands, pages 52–53, for this technique). Add a gold bucket (template on page 58) to the base with foam pads. Mount onto green patterned paper and then a green card blank.

Tip . . .

Paper with any
pattern can be used for
framing the main panel;
it doesn't have to be
especially festive. But don't
worry if you haven't got any
green patterned paper –
you can
just omit it.

# FINISHING THE CARD

Glue the pears onto red card where the ball of tree foliage will be, making sure that they are evenly spaced – it's best to position them first with some leaves before gluing in place. Arrange the gold-edged and plain green leaves around the pears and glue on, placing some at an angle to give dimension and texture to the tree. Use scallop-edged scissors to cut a trunk from gold card and then wrap the ribbon around, securing it on the reverse of the trunk. Mount onto the red card with foam pads. Cut a pot shape from gold card using the template on page 58, tie ribbon around it in a bow and mount onto the red card using foam pads. Mount the red card to a larger rectangle of green patterned paper and then to a green card blank.

# TRIANGLE TREE

A triangle is cut from green card and a pot from gold card using the templates on page 59. Three pears are glued to the triangle, with a fourth at the top, and the areas around the pears filled in with 18 leaves. The tree is then glued to red card. Green organza ribbon is tied around the pot and then mounted below the tree with foam pads. A strip of green patterned paper is glued onto a green card blank and then the red card mounted on top.

# POINSETTIA POSY

The poinsettia has a long association with Christmas and is a popular decorative feature in the home, the vibrant reds and greens of the plant's star-shaped leaves complementing the traditional colour scheme of the festive season. Here, narrower paper than usual is used for the quilled petal shapes so that the 'flowers' (which are actually leaf bunches) can be constructed from two layers without being overly bulky. Two poinsettia blooms can look equally effective, or a single bloom makes an elegant statement, as shown in the variations. Poinsettias do vary in colour, depending on the variety, so you could make white or pink flowers instead.

You will need....

- papers: 5mm (3/16in) wide light green; 3mm (1/8in) wide dark green; 2mm (1/16in) wide red
- card: cream, green
- dark green card blank
- yellow 3D paint

1 Make five tight coils with 1.5cm (5/8in) lengths of the 5mm (3/16in) wide light green paper. Trim two of these coils by about 1.5mm (1/16in).

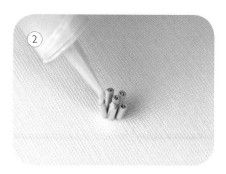

2 Glue these coils to the cream card where the centre of the flower is to be, ensuring that you leave enough space for the leaves and petals. Put dots of yellow 3D paint on the ends of each of the green coils – it's best to squirt the paint onto scrap paper first to get it flowing. Leave to dry.

3 For the two green leaves, make loose closed coils from 40cm (15 3/4in) lengths of the 3mm (1/8in) wide dark green paper and pinch at both ends. Glue either side of the centre coils. For the red petals (per flower), you will need pinched coils made from the following: two 40cm (15 3/4in), two 60cm (23 3/4in) and three 80cm (32in) lengths of 2mm (1/16in) red paper for the lower layer; two 30cm (12in), one 40cm (15 3/4in), two 60cm (23 3/4in) and three 80cm (32in) lengths for the top layer.

SENTIMENT SUGGESTIONS

May Your Christmas Be Merry and Bright

Wishing You a Wonderful Holiday

Thinking of You This Christmastime

Warm Wishes This Christmas

## SINGLE POINSETTIA

Here, a single poinsettia 'flower' is mounted onto a circle of light green card. A notch is cut in the spine of a darker green card blank through which green organza ribbon is then threaded. The ribbon is tied in a knot around the front of the card and the poinsettia mounted on top of the ribbon. A Christmas greeting could be added if you wish. The circle with the bloom attached could alternatively be used as a gift tag, with a hole punched in it threaded with ribbon.

Tip . . .

The 3D paint needs at least an hour to dry, so it's best to make these flowers in two stages. If you don't have 3D paint, you can use yellow acrylic paint instead.

## FINISHING THE CARD

As there are two layers of petals to each poinsettia, it's a good idea to try out their positioning first until you are happy with the arrangement before gluing in place. Once one poinsettia has been glued to the cream card, make two more poinsettias in the same way and glue in place. Mount the cream card to green card and then to a dark green card blank.

## CLEAN AND CONTEMPORARY

The traditional poinsettia flower can also be made into a contemporary-style card by teaming it with bright colours and keeping the design clean-cut. Here, a single quilled bloom is mounted onto a square of ivory card without any leaves to keep the outline of the shape simple. A length of pink card is scored and folded so that the front panel is smaller than the back panel. Green spotted paper is trimmed with scallop-edged scissors and attached to the inside back panel of the pink card. The ivory square is then mounted with foam pads onto the front of the pink card.

# Funky Tree

The quilling technique can be used to great effect as a highlight in a card design. Here, quilled coils add interest to a foam pad-mounted cut-out tree, set into punched holes so that they are flush with the surface. This is a quick card to make and is therefore an ideal candidate for batch production when several can be made in one sitting, proving that not all quilled cards take time to make! Variations on the basic design are just as speedy and eye-catching.

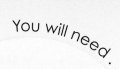

You will need....

- papers: 3mm (1/8in) pinks, red
- card: light green, red, bright pink
- light pink card blank
- small circle punches: 3mm (1/8in) and 6mm (1/4in) in diameter

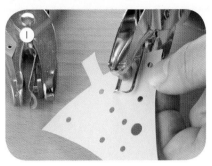

1 Use the template on page 58 to cut out a tree from light green card. Use the two sizes of small circle punch to make holes in the tree shape where indicated on the template; the template is a guide only.

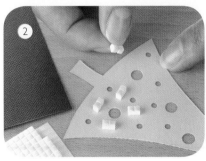

2 Place mini foam pads in between the holes on the tree, ensuring that they are positioned all over the shape, but not too close to the edges. Remove the backing from the foam pads and mount onto red card.

3 Using a quilling tool, make a loose coil with a 7cm (2 3/4in) length of the pink paper. Apply glue to one side of the coil, insert into one of the larger holes in the tree and allow to unravel slightly in the hole. Then take a 3cm (1 1/4in) length of the red paper and make a loose coil, then glue as before and insert into a smaller hole.

### Tip . . .

If making multiples of this speedy design, cut out all the tree shapes, then punch all the holes and finally insert the coils.

## Stripy Tree

Striped paper in a striking contrast of varying pinks and greens is used as a lively backdrop to the lime green tree. The colours of the coils have then been chosen to echo the different shades of pink in the patterned paper. Any patterned paper can be used as a background, but make sure that it isn't too dominant or it will overwhelm the quilled tree. A larger card could be made with three trees of differing colours in a row.

**Tip . . .**

You can vary the size of the tree shape used. If making a larger tree, use an 'anywhere' hole punch so that you can reach the centre of the tree.

# FINISHING THE CARD

Use different shades of pink and the red paper to make enough loose coils to fill all the holes in the tree. Mount the red card onto bright pink card and then onto a light pink card blank. For a very modern take on this design, choose a shocking pink or bright red for the tree with contrasting coils, such as gold- or silver-edged white, set into the punched holes. You could also add presents to the card – see pages 46–47 for instructions.

# PINK PINE

This vibrant variation on the main design features hues of pink and green for a clean, contemporary feel. The tree is cut from light pink card and mounted onto a rectangle of deeper pink card, which in turn is mounted onto a red card blank. Two shades of green 3mm (1/8in) paper are used to make the loose coils that fill the holes in the tree. Finally, the card is finished with pink ribbon tied in a bow around the card. The colours can be varied, but stick to complementary ones.

# DOVE OF PEACE

Traditionally a symbol of peace, the dove is a favourite motif for Christmas and New Year cards. Here, ivory papers with a gold edge are used to bring a light-catching highlight to this special messenger. The bird's swirling tail is made using lengths of paper folded and formed into open coils, and a double layer of coils for the wings enhances the effect of being in flight. By using one shade of colour for the dove, the focus is concentrated on its outline and texture to create a striking image for a symbolic statement.

You will need.....

- papers: 3mm (1/8in) wide gold-edged ivory, black
- purple card
- ivory card blank
- transfer lettering or computer-generated lettering
- decorative-edged scissors

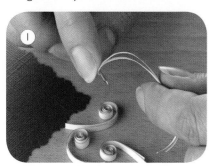

1 Cut a square of purple card with decorative-edged scissors. Fold a 15cm (6in) length of the gold-edged ivory paper in half. Using a needle tool, coil the folded end of the paper around the tool and continue coiling to the end of the paper. Remove the tool and let the coil unwind. Make seven more of these open double coils. Glue together at the non-coiled ends for the tail.

2 For the body and wings, using a quilling tool, make a large number of loose closed coils with 15cm (6in) lengths of the gold-edged ivory paper and pinch one end into a point to create teardrops. For the eye, glue a 2.5cm (1in) length of the black paper onto a 15cm (6in) length of gold-edged ivory paper. Make a coil starting with the black paper and glue at the end of the black paper, then carry on coiling until the end of the gold-edged ivory paper and glue in place. Glue in position on the purple card before gluing on any of the other coils.

3 Build up the bird shape on the purple card with the teardrop shapes, pinching some into leaf shapes as you go. Create the beak by making a loose closed coil from a 15cm (6in) length of the paper and pinching into a triangle shape. For the wing, add a second layer of teardrop shapes on top of the first.

## DIMINUTIVE DOVE

The main card uses a lot of coils, so for a quicker version the dove can be scaled down in size, thereby requiring fewer coils. The paper used here is copper-edged ivory, which gives a warm feel and works well with the mauve background. All the elements of the dove use the same measurements as for the main design. The head and beak are made first, then glued in place on the card. The body is formed from 15 eye-shaped coils; arrange them first, and when you are happy with the layout, glue them in place. The tail is made following Step 1 of the main card with five open coils glued together and attached to the body. The first wing consists of about nine teardrop shapes glued directly to the card, with another seven for the second wing, glued on top of the first.

Peace and Goodwill

**Tip . . .**

You can colour the edges of plain papers with a gold pen or gold paint instead, but at this busy time it's best not to create work for yourself, and ready-gilded strips do have a better finish.

# Finishing the Card

When the dove is complete, mount the purple card onto an ivory card blank. Add a suitable greeting such as 'Peace and Goodwill' using transfer lettering or a computer-generated message. This is a project where you could make the teardrop shapes in spare moments and store in a container until you are ready to assemble the final card. As all the shapes use the same length of paper, it's easy to cut strips in advance and coil when time allows. Also, it isn't necessary for the coiled shapes to be all exactly the same size, as when you come to assemble the dove it will add variety if they are not uniform.

# On the Wing

As well as being a Biblical symbol of peace, a dove in flight with an olive branch in its beak gives movement to this variation on the main design. Here, the wings are either side of the main body and consist of a double layer of coils, as in the main card, with gold-edged ivory paper used throughout. The body consists of nine coils and then each wing has eight teardrops, with six on the lower layer and two on top. Open coils are made for the tail as before. For the olive branch, four leaf shapes are made from 5cm (2in) lengths of 3mm (1/8in) wide green paper and glued either side of a 2.5cm (1in) length of the paper (see Gilded Garlands, pages 52–53). The word 'love' is added to the purple background, but this could be any festive message.

LOVE

# BEAUTIFUL BAUBLES

The quilling technique of husking is another way in which strips of coloured paper can be used to handcraft intriguing, intricately formed decorative shapes. The paper is simply wrapped around an arrangement of pins inserted into a foam block, and by using a template for the positioning of the pins, the same shape can be made numerous times. When this technique is combined with metallic-edged papers, the results make fabulous festive baubles.

## You will need . . . .

- papers: 3mm (1/8in) wide gold-edged orange, orange, gold-edged pink, pink
- card: pink, mauve, silver, orange
- orange card blank
- gold ribbon
- transfer lettering
- foam block and pins
- masking tape
- emery board

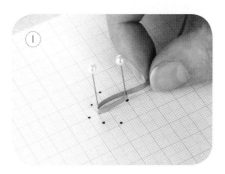

1 Trace or photocopy the template on page 61. Place the template on a foam block and hold in place with masking tape. Insert two pins through the paper and into the foam block at the points marked 1 and 2. Take a length of the gold-edged orange paper, fold over one end and loop around pin 1. Take the other end around pin 2. Add a dot of glue at this end and secure the paper to it.

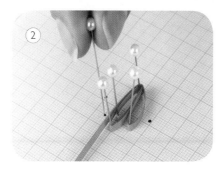

2 Insert a pin above the top pin at point 3, wrap the paper around this pin and then take it back to the base pin 1. Add a dot of glue at the base. Insert a pin at point 4, wrap the paper around this pin, then take it back to pin 1. The photo shows the paper being looped around pin 5.

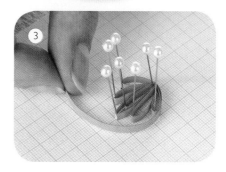

3 Continue in this way with pin 6 and pin 7. Then take the length of paper all the way round the outside of the pins and back to the base. Glue the paper in place and trim the end. Remove the pins from the foam block and put the shape to one side. Make another shape in the same way. See page 61 for detailed illustrations on how to make the husking shapes.

## Tip . . .

Instead of foam board, you can use a piece of polystyrene salvaged from packaging.

## BAUBLE WINDOW

Here, a circle aperture is cut into a purple card blank, and a bauble shape cut from orange card and given a silver top, which is then suspended in the aperture by a length of thread. Three husking shapes are made from purple paper as in the main card and glued to the orange bauble. Three teardrop shapes are made from 10cm (4in) lengths of mauve paper and each inserted into a husking shape. A purple gemstone is then glued to the centre of the motif. For the corner decoration, groups of three teardrop shapes are also made from 10cm (4in) lengths of the purple paper with a gemstone added to the centre of each.

## And Finally...

Glue the four shapes to the centre of the pink bauble as shown in the photo. Make teardrop shapes from 10cm (4in) lengths of the plain orange paper (see page 12) and glue to the centre of each husking shape. Make a small coil from a 15cm (6in) length of the gold-edged orange paper and glue to the centre of the shape. For the mauve bauble, make four husking shapes in the same way but using gold-edged pink paper and taking the paper all the way around the outside to finish for each one. Add teardrops in plain pink paper and a centre coil in gold-edged pink paper. Use transfer letting to add 'Seasons Greetings' to a strip of orange card and mount using foam pads.

## Finishing the Card

Make two more shapes, but finish after looping the paper around pin 7 without taking the paper right the way around the outside. Using the templates on page 60, cut two bauble shapes from pink and mauve card and use an emery board to sand the edges. Use the templates to cut two bauble tops from silver card and glue to the baubles. Mount these onto an orange card blank using foam pads. Tie gold ribbon to the top of each bauble, hang over the top of the card and secure on the reverse side.

## Eastern Star

A tall bauble is cut from pink card, mounted onto a light pink background and given a silver top decorated with a pink ribbon bow. Four husking shapes are made as in the main card using light purple paper and then glued to the bauble. Teardrop shapes made using 10cm (4in) strips of pink paper are then inserted into the centre of each husking shape and a clear gemstone added to the centre and secured with strong glue. The pink card is then mounted onto a darker pink card blank.

# CRYSTAL SNOWFLAKE

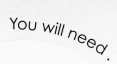

You will need . . . .

- paper: 3mm (1/8in) wide white
- blue card
- tall blue card blank
- 6mm (1/4in) and 3mm (1/8in) Swarovski crystals
- strong glue

Authentic Swarovski crystals in two different sizes are combined with elegant white coils for this sophisticated snowflake motif. The crystals are set into the coils so that they become an integral part of the design, adding sparkle and style, illustrating yet another dimension that quilling can take. While the snowflake is rendered in realistic white paper, its form is given a more cutting-edge, abstract treatment by being only partially pictured.

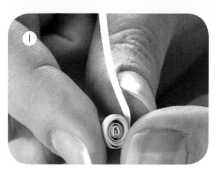

1 Using a quilling tool, take a 25cm (10in) length of the white paper and coil 15cm (6in) of it. Release the coil a little and then glue, leaving a 'tail' of 10cm (4in) of the paper hanging loose.

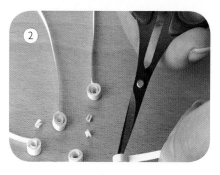

2 Use the points of a pair of fine-tipped scissors to cut out the centre of the coil, taking care to cut out the very centre of the coil only. Make three more coils and cut out the centre of each in the same way. Glue the coils to a piece of blue card to form the tips of the snowflake.

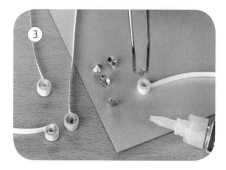

3 Use fine-tipped tweezers to hold a large crystal, apply a dot of strong glue to the reverse of the crystal and then insert it into the hole of the coil, point first. Release the tweezers and, using your fingertip, press the crystal into the coil, taking care not to get any glue on your fingers.

### Tip . . .

A word or sentiment could be added in quilled letters, such as 'Snow' – see Festive Fonts, pages 34–35.

## DIAMOND DAZZLE

This smaller snowflake, mounted onto a square of blue card positioned diamond style, uses the same measurements as for the main card except that the 'prongs' are only 5cm (2in) long. Large blue crystals are set into the outer coils and the centre coil, with smaller blue crystals set into pairs of teardrops on each 'prong'. Small clear crystals are set into bent teardrop shapes positioned either side of each outermost coil. Any colour of crystal can be used, but make sure that they coordinate with the card you use as a background. Clear crystals are neutral, so will complement any colour scheme.

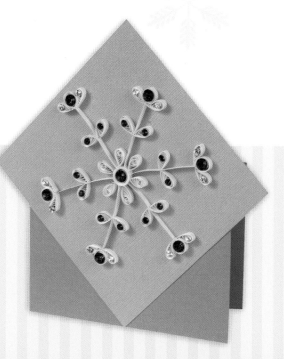

**Tip . . .**

If you don't have crystals, you can use flat-backed gemstones instead. Be sure to use strong glue to secure any gemstones, otherwise they will drop off the card.

# Finishing the Card

Make a loose closed coil from a 25cm (10in) length of the white paper, cut the centre out as before and then glue to the blue card where you want the centre of the snowflake to be. Glue a large crystal in the centre of the coil. Glue the end of the 'tail' of one of the coils previously glued in place to the centre coil, then repeat for the remaining three outer coils. Make teardrop-shaped coils from 10cm (4in) lengths of white paper (see page 12), snip the centres out and glue around the centre coil, point outwards. Insert small crystals into the coils. To complete the 'prongs' of the snowflake, make bent teadrop coils from 10cm (4in) lengths of the paper (see page 12), glue point inwards in pairs to the 'tail' and insert small crystals.

# Flake Fragment

Here, just three snowflake 'prongs' adorn an ice blue card tag for a speedy design. The tag is mounted onto snowflake-patterned vellum, which is attached with four white brads to a blue card blank. A loose closed coil is made with white paper, then the centre cut out following Step 2 of the main design. This is glued to the left-hand side of the blue tag. Three coils with tails are made as in Step 1 of the main card but with shorter tails of 5cm (2in). The coils are glued to the blue tag as shown and then four large clear crystals glued into the centre of each coil. Three teardrop shapes made from 10cm (4in) lengths of white paper are attached around the central coil, point inwards.

# FESTIVE FONTS

Quilling is a wonderful way to coil and curl paper strips into letters and numbers for cards and tags, to personalize them and add any special message you wish. Here, 5mm (3/16in) wide paper is used for the all-important date to make it stand out more prominently. The other letters all use 3mm (1/8in) wide paper to create a fancy script. The finishing touch is the snow effect on the numbers and letters, produced using Flower Soft®, which is a light, feathery substance that is easily glued to paper.

## You will need....

- papers: 5mm (3/16in) wide red; 3mm (1/8in) wide red
- card: green, red
- red single-fold card, 9cm x 15cm (3 1/2 x 6in)
- white Flower Soft®
- fine needle set into a cork
- tacky glue

1 Cut a circle 7.5cm (3in) in diameter from green card. To make the '2', use a 20cm (8in) length of the 5mm (3/16in) red paper and coil both ends into open coils with the fine needle and cork. Crease the paper to create the main shape of the number and glue to the green card circle, applying a dot of glue under each coil and the crease of the number.

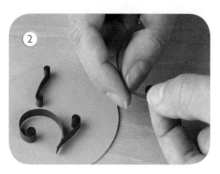

2 For the '5', coil a 7cm (2 3/4in) length of the red paper at both ends using the needle and cork to form a scroll shape. Crease a 15cm (6in) length for the upright of the '5' and coil the other end. Use a fingernail to curl the paper into a nice curve. Glue to the green card circle next to the '2'.

3 Cut a small circle from green card 2.5cm (1in) in diameter. Make a 't' from a 3cm (1 1/4in) and 2cm (3/4in) length of the 3mm (1/8in) red paper. The 'h' is a 5cm (2in) length. For the letters, use the following lengths of the 3mm (1/8in) red paper: D = 5cm (2in) and 10cm (4in), e = 9cm (3 1/2in), c = 6cm 2 3/8in), m = 10cm (4in), b = 12cm (4 3/4in) and r = 7cm (2 3/4in). Apply the tacky glue to the tops of the numbers and letters. Hold the card over scrap paper or a container and sprinkle the Flower Soft® over the glue. Gently shake off the excess and leave to dry.

## MERRY MESSAGE

Any festive message can be spelled out using quilled letters, but for longer messages it is best to use narrower strips of paper, enabling you to make smaller letters, so that they will fit onto regular card sizes. Here, the greeting 'Merry Christmas' is formed using 2mm (1/16in) wide red paper mounted onto bright green card, then topped with white Flower Soft®. In two corners sprigs of holly (see pages 40–41) add a finishing touch. The following lengths of the red paper are used for the letters: M = 20cm (8in); e, r, y = 9cm (3 1/2in) each; C = 15cm (6in); h, r, s, a = 9cm (3 1/2in) each; i = 6cm (2 3/8in) with 3cm (1 1/4in) for the dot; t = 7cm (2 3/4in) with a 3cm (1 1/4in) scroll for the cross piece; m = 10cm (4in).

Tip . . .

Here, a fine needle set into a cork is used to achieve a smaller centre to the coil and to avoid the kink that the quilling tool leaves. However, this only affects the fine detail and you can use a quilling tool if you prefer.

## FINISHING THE CARD

Mount the green card circle to the red single-fold card so that the circle is positioned halfway over the top of the card. Attach the smaller circle with the 'th' next to the larger circle. Add a strip of green card 3cm x 15cm (1 1/4 x 6in) with the 'December' below the circles and then add another plain strip of green card 1cm x 15cm (3/8in x 6in) below this. When using quilling for script, it's best to plan the letters in advance, to check that they will fit the space you have. It's a good idea to begin by gluing the first letter and last letter in place, then work inwards. So in this case, first glue on the 'D' and 'r' of December and then add the other letters.

## CHRISTMAS EVE GREETING

The night before Christmas is celebrated here in quilled red numbers and letters, given the same 'snow' treatment as before. Card circles are cut from green card and the number '2' and 'th' created as for the main design. The number '4' consists of a 15cm (6in) length of red paper for the main part and then 2cm (3/4in) and 3cm (1 1/4in) lengths for the two vertical pieces either side of the horizontal piece. For the 'ho's, the 'h' is a single 18cm (7in) length of paper folded and then glued and coiled. The 'o's are 10cm (4in) lengths coiled at one end and the non-coiled end then glued to the coil. The 'ho's are mounted onto a strip of green card and then a red card blank with the fold at the top. The two card circles are glued so that they extend above the fold.

# DING-DONG MERRILY

You will need....

In most villages in the past, the church bell was rung to mark any important event, including in celebration of Christmas. In this design, each quilled bell is made from one long length of gold paper formed into a dome shape and a small black tight coil with a tail for the clanger hanging down from the inside. Although highly realistic in effect, the fir branches are really quick to create using short lengths of green paper glued to a central paper stem.

- papers: 3mm (1/8in) wide green, gold-edged gold; 2mm (1/16in) wide black
- light green card
- clear patterned vellum
- green tall card blank

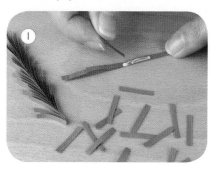

1 For the fir branches, begin by cutting lots of 2cm (3/4in) lengths of the green paper. Place glue on the end of a 7cm (2 3/4in) length of the green paper for the central stem. Put a 2cm (3/4in) strip on the end, then place another small strip just next to it. Continue adding 2cm (3/4in) strips all the way along the stem and then repeat for the other side.

2 Glue several strips of the gold paper end to end to form one 140cm (55in) length, make into a tight coil using a quilling tool and glue the end in place. Remove the quilling tool and then push the centre of the coil up with your finger to make a dome shape. Put glue inside the bell to hold its shape and leave to dry. Add a very small loop to the top of the bell.

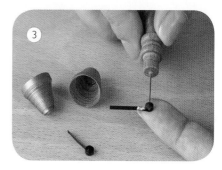

3 For the bell clanger, cut a 15cm (6in) length of the black paper and coil tightly with the quilling tool until you are 1.5cm (5/8in) from the end. Glue the coil without releasing it so that you have a tight coil with a 'tail'. Glue the tail to the inside top of the bell shape.

SENTIMENT SUGGESTIONS

Ring Out the Bells

The Bells in Heaven are Ringing

Jingle all the Way

'Tis the Season to be Jolly

Deck the Halls!

## CHRISTMAS BELL TRIO

For this striking design, three bells hang from a fir branch descending in height to the bottom right of the deep red card. Gold thread has been tied through the tiny loop on the top of each bell and then around the fir branch, but the bells are also glued to the card. A subsidiary fir branch is glued to the main top branch so that it hangs downwards, and another two small fir branches added to the bottom right-hand side of the card. Finally, 'Noel' is added with gold transfer lettering.

Tip . . .

When pushing up the tight coil to make a dome shape, instead of your finger you could use a mould, such as a lid, as in Mistletoe Wishes, pages 18–19.

## Finishing the Card

Glue three sets of two bells to a rectangle of light green card, with two fir branches over each set to give the appearance of hanging bells. Mount the panel onto clear patterned vellum – in this case printed with the words of the well-loved carol 'While Shepherds Watch Their Flocks by Night', but any festive-patterned vellum or white paper could be used. Finally, attach to a tall green card blank.

## Window Bells

As the quilled bells are entirely three-dimensional, they are ideally suited to being hung freely. So for this card a circle aperture is cut in a green card blank within which to suspend a duo of bells. 'Merry Christmas' is added with transfer lettering, but a handwritten greeting in black pen could be used instead. Seven fir branches are glued to the card to frame the bell aperture and give a luxuriant foliage effect. Although the background card colour is also green, the shade is a good contrast against the quilled fir branches.

# Simply Stockings

The sight of stockings hanging in a row is enough to fill anyone's heart with expectations of lovely surprises to come. Time is a precious commodity at Christmas, and while the pressure is on to produce cards quickly, it doesn't mean that you have to leave out the quilling, as this fast and festive design proves. The stockings are decorated with just a hint of quilling, but being worked in white, it has great impact against the red card. This would be ideal for an anniversary card – especially to celebrate three years of marriage!

**You will need....**

- papers: 3mm (1/8in) wide white; 2mm (1/16in) wide white
- card: red, white
- red card blank
- mini wooden pegs
- green ribbon
- quilling board (optional)

1 Take a 20cm (8in) length of the 3mm (1/8in) white paper and make a loose closed coil, preferably using a quilling board – although its use is optional, it will ensure that your coils are all identical. Pinch one end into a point to make a teardrop shape. Make another teardrop in the same way.

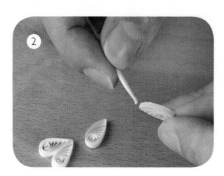

2 Apply glue to one edge of the pinched coil and then press the other teardrop shape onto the glue to join together, forming a heart. Make two more hearts in the same way. Using the template on page 60, cut three stockings and tops from red card. Glue the tops to the stockings, then glue a heart to the centre of each stocking.

3 For the trim on the stockings, cut 2.5cm (1in) lengths of the 2mm (1/16in) wide white paper. Using the quilling tool, coil one end towards the centre of the strip, turn around and coil the other end to the centre to make an 's'-shaped open scroll. Glue to the edge of the stocking top. Each stocking uses six scrolls.

**Tip . . .**

Patterned cardstock can be used for the stockings, but make sure it's subtle enough not to overwhelm the quilling.

# Christmas Countdown

For a fun card that counts down to the big day, a red stocking is decorated with pink scrolls around the top and a pink heart, and a small paper loop glued to the top. It's then attached to a pink card blank with foam pads and a mini wooden peg added to hold the loop to the top edge of the card. Numbers are printed on white paper using a home computer, then cut out individually and secured to green card with a brad in each top corner. All 25 numbers can be printed, but it may be best to do just 20–25. A decorative border is added around the green card and attached to top right of the pink card. A slit is cut in the card spine, threaded with organza ribbon and tied in a bow below the stocking. The words 'days to go' are printed onto pink card and secured over the ribbon.

Tip . . .

There are many shades of white, so make sure that the white you use for the quilling matches the white of the card background.

# FINISHING THE CARD

Glue three mini wooden pegs to a piece of white card, then thread a length of green ribbon through the pegs and tie in a knot at each end. Clip a stocking into each peg to look as though they are hanging. To ensure that the stockings don't fall out in transit, add a mini foam pad under each to secure. Mount the white card onto a red card blank.

# GREAT EXPECTATIONS

Here, three stockings and tops are cut from pink, green and red card, and assembled with contrasting-coloured tops. White quilled scrolls are made as in the main design and glued to the red and green stocking tops, with deep pink scrolls added to the pink top. The same heart decorations featured in the main card are used to jolly up each stocking, two white for the pink and red stockings and one pink for the green stocking. The green stocking is glued directly to a rectangle of white card, while foam pads are used to mount the other two stockings. The white card is mounted onto red card and then a pink card blank with the fold at the top. Finally, a bough of festive fir (see page 36 for how to make) is glued across the top of all three stockings.

Simply Stockings  **39**

# Holly Wreath

Being one of the few plants able to thrive in harsh conditions, holly once signified hope and life in the darkness of winter. Today, it is an important feature of festive decorations, with its distinctive spiky, glossy, dark green leaves. Here, these have been rendered in a stylized form using pinched quilled coils and arranged fanning outwards to create a ring, built up in layers. The wreath is topped with a gold ribbon bow and small green gemstones set in the leaves to add a hint of sparkle.

1 Take a 40cm (15 3/4in) length of the dark green paper and make it into a loose closed coil. Holding the centre of the coil with the fingertips of one hand, pinch the tip of the coil with your other hand.

## Tip . . .

For a quicker version of the main wreath, just make one layer of holly leaves around the circle, as in Step 3.

2 Turn the coil around and, holding the centre of the coil with the fingertips of one hand, pinch the other tip of the coil with your other hand. You will now have a squeezed shape, so use tweezers to hold the centre and gently push the ends inwards to 'plump' the shape. Make lots of holly leaves in the same way, varying their size and shape slightly so that they are not uniform.

3 As a guide to shaping your wreath, place the circle of scrap card in the centre of a square of red card and hold in place with low-tack tape underneath. Position holly leaves around the circle so that they point out at 45 degrees, then glue them in place.

## Holly Spray

A quilled holly spray makes a stylish motif for a quick card. Here, 11 holly leaves are set along one main paper stem and a side shoot (see Gilded Garlands, pages 52–53 for this technique) against a light green background, with three red tight coils made from 10cm (4in) red paper for berries. The word 'Noel' is added with transfer lettering just below the branch. A slightly larger red card panel to which the light green card is mounted picks up the colour of the berries, and this in turn is mounted onto a green card blank with the fold at the top. Dark green organza ribbon is threaded through the fold and around the card, then tied in knot.

**Tip . . .**

When starting a project that needs a lot of shapes of one colour, do a quick check to make sure you have enough paper before you begin.

# Finishing the Card

Once the initial circle of holly leaves has been glued in place, remove the card circle. Continue to build up the wreath by adding more holly leaves outwards and then another layer on top. Some leaves are glued at a slight angle on the top layer to add some dimension. Add the green gemstones to the wreath, or you could use red berries instead (see the Holly Spray variation opposite). Tie the gold ribbon in a bow and attach to the holly wreath, then mount the red card to squares of green card in two slightly different sizes and shades using green brads and finally onto a dark green card blank.

# Holly Sprigs

Just nine holly leaves are needed for this super-speedy design. The leaves are grouped in threes on mauve card, with a red gemstone in the centre of each group to add sparkle, although you could use a red tight coil instead. 'Christmas Greetings' is printed onto a mauve card strip and then mounted below the holly with foam pads. The mauve card is then mounted onto red card and then a green card blank. A single group of three holly leaves would make a pretty matching tag.

# Speedy Snowflake

Snowflakes are naturally suited to the medium of quilling. Elegant white paper coils can be arranged in a limitless number of ways so that no two quilled snowflakes need be the same. However, when things are hectic in the run-up to Christmas, time is of the essence and this snowflake design has been especially designed for mass production. Open coils are teamed with teardrop shapes to build up the 'prongs' of the snowflake for a beautifully delicate yet speedy effect.

You will need . . . .

- paper: 2mm (1/16in) wide white
- dark blue card circle 7.5cm (3in) in diameter
- bright blue card blank
- blue organza ribbon

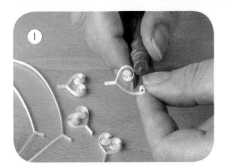

1 Take a 15cm (6in) length of the white paper and fold it in half to find the centre. Add glue to the centre 5mm (3/16in) of the length and press the glued sides together. Use a quilling tool to coil each end towards the centre fold. Make five more of these shapes in the same way.

2 Use the quilling tool to make a tight coil from a 15cm (6in) length of the white paper. Find the centre of the blue card circle and glue the coil to the centre. Glue the six shapes made in Step 1 around the centre coil as shown. Using the quilling tool, make loose closed coils from 15cm (6in) lengths of the white paper and pinch at either end into leaf shapes. Glue close to the top of the open coils.

3 Make six more leaf shapes of the same size. Glue these next to the centre coil in between the stems of the open coils.

SENTIMENT SUGGESTIONS

Have a Sparkling Christmas

Warmest Winter Wishes to You

May all Your Christmas Wishes Come True

Let it Snow!

## Snow Fall

This design uses opaque plastic to create an airy feeling of a falling snowflake. A circle aperture is cut into a dark turquoise card using a circle cutter and template, and opaque plastic attached behind with double-sided tape. A tight coil is made from a 15cm (6in) length of the white paper and attached to the centre using regular glue. Six white eye shapes are made from 15cm (6in) lengths and glued evenly around the central coil. Next, a 15cm (6in) length is folded in half and then each end coiled inwards to the centre fold to make a heart. Five more hearts are made and glued folded-point inwards between the coils. Finally, six more eye shapes are glued with the points inserted into the tops of the hearts.

Tip . . .

All snowflakes have six 'prongs' and it's important that they align exactly with each other, otherwise the motif will look unbalanced.

# Finishing the Card

Attach the card circle to the top of a bright blue card blank. Thread blue organza ribbon through the spine of the card and tie in a bow on the right-hand side, trimming the ends if necessary. You could add a greeting if you wish. It's easy to experiment and increase the diameter of the snowflake by adding more leaf shapes or open coils, so you may want to sketch out an idea that would need a larger circle of card. Snowflakes vary greatly and you will find a wide range of styles and shapes to inspire your card designs in books or on the internet.

# Snowflake Cameo

In this variation design, a snowflake is mounted onto a circle of red card and then attached to a blue card blank with the fold at the top. The snowflake is begun as before with a tight coil in the centre, then six eye shapes are glued around this central coil. A 15cm (6in) length of the white paper is folded in half and then glued together for about 5mm (3/16in) along from the fold. The ends are then coiled away and outwards from the central fold (as opposed to the main card where they are coiled inwards to the centre). Five more shapes are made in the same way and then the folded ends glued to the central coil and the coiled ends above the eye shapes. Finally, six more eye shapes are made and glued point inwards in between the open coils.

# BERRY MERRY

The glorious natural colours of the winter season are celebrated here in bountiful sprigs of luscious red berries and glossy deep green leaves set against a warm, earthy-coloured background. The rounded shape of the berries is created by pushing up the centres of quilled coils, and brown paper stems and sepals added for extra realism. Silver glitter glue on the berries enhances the 3D effect, as well giving them, and the leaves, a festive sparkle.

## You will need....

- papers: 3mm (1/8in) wide red, brown, dark green
- beige card blank
- silver glitter glue
- transfer lettering or black pen
- sheet of acetate

1 For the berries, use a quilling tool to make a tight coil with a 40cm (15 3/4in) length of the red paper. Glue the end in place and remove the quilling tool. Use the tip of your finger to push up the centre of the coil to make an even dome shape. Make tight coils using four 40cm (15 3/4in), five 60cm (23 3/4in) and seven 80cm (32in) lengths of red paper.

2 Use a cocktail stick (toothpick) to apply a generous amount of glue inside the quilled dome shapes and place on a sheet of acetate, glue side down (using acetate enables the berries to be removed easily once dry). Add silver glitter glue to one half of a dome shape only, using a fresh cocktail stick (toothpick). Repeat for all the dome shapes and then leave to dry.

3 To make stems for the berries, glue two 40cm (15 3/4in) lengths of the brown paper together and leave to dry, then cut in half lengthways. For the berry sepals, take a 3cm (1 1/4in) length of the same paper and fringe one end using fine-tipped scissors. Glue the stem to the side of the berry where the silver glitter is, and glue the non-fringed end of the sepal to the berry on the opposite side to the stem. Repeat for all the berries.

## Tip . . .

The silver glitter glue doesn't have to be used, as plain berries and leaves also look festive.

# BERRY WREATH

A simple but luxurious wreath of red berries is mounted onto cream card, then attached to a brown card blank with brown brads. The berries are made in the same way as for the main card from 20cm (8in), 40cm (15 3/4in), 60cm (23 3/4in) and 80cm (32in) lengths of red 3mm (1/8in) wide paper, given sepals but not stems and then highlighted with glitter glue. They are then arranged in a circle (see page 40 for this technique), with some glued on their side to enhance the wreath effect. Gold ribbon tied in a bow is then added for a finishing touch.

Tip . . .

Sprigs of these leaves
and berries could
be arranged over or
around an aperture
in a card blank, such
as in the Window Bells
design on page 37.

# FINISHING THE CARD

Glue the stalks of the berries together in varying groups, as shown, then glue
in place on the card blank, with some berries glued on their edge overlapping
other berries. For the leaves, form twenty 40cm (15 3/4in) lengths of the dark
green paper into loose closed coils and then pinch into teardrop shapes (see
page 12). Attach to strips of the same paper and then arrange on the card.
Add silver glitter glue to the tips of the leaves. Finally, use transfer lettering or a
black pen to add a greeting such as 'Merry Christmas'.

# BERRY TAG

For a quicker version of the main card, a single sprig of red berries is mounted
onto a tag of patterned card. The berries and leaves are made as for the main
card, but the leaves are not glittered. A band of brown card with scalloped
edges is mounted across a beige card blank, and then the tag attached with
foam pads on top. The tag is then threaded with two pieces of warm brown
ribbon. The tag could be used on its own as a gift tag.

# PRESENT PERFECT

Giving and receiving presents is a key aspect of Christmas, so a generous stack of colourful gifts makes a great image for a card. This design again shows that a single simple quilled feature – in this case the bows – is enough to make it stand out from the crowd. The cute mini presents that the quilled bows adorn are quickly made from paper, and the array of vibrant colours set against a white card blank will bring lots of festive cheer to the recipient. This card could easily be adapted for a birthday – ideal for a shopaholic! Alternatively, a single present on a tag could be used for a real gift.

1 The coils for the bows need to be of equal size, so a quilling board is used here. Using a quilling tool, make a coil from a 20cm (8in) length of the red paper, place glue on the end and then put into a circle template on the board, allowing the coil to unwind to the edge of the circle. Remove from the board and pinch one end while using your fingernail to push in the other end. Make another three pinched shapes in the same way.

2 Take a 3cm (1 1/4in) length of the red paper and roll around a tool, such as the end of an embossing tool as used here, then glue the end in place. Slide off the tool for a perfect circle.

### Tip . . .

Just one of these presents with a quilled bow on a tag could make an eye-catching Christmas card.

3 Cover a piece of scrap card with pink giftwrapping paper and secure on the reverse side. Wrap two lengths of the red paper around the square, vertically and horizontally, and tape to the reverse. Glue the circle made in Step 2 to the centre and then glue on two pinched shapes, points inwards. Glue the other two shapes in between.

## GIFT GRID

A grid format is used for this design, where four presents are set on a green square card blank. The pink and mauve presents are topped with bows as for the main card with colours chosen to harmonize together. When arranging the gifts in a group, they need to be positioned close together with just a small gap in between. The grid layout could be extended to nine presents (three by three), or you can make a horizontal or vertical row of just three gifts if you are short of time.

Tip . . .

When making mini presents, the covering paper needs to be relatively thin, otherwise it will be too bulky, so wrapping paper is the ideal choice.

# FINISHING THE CARD

Make the other presents in the same way, using green paper to make a bow for the light green giftwrapping paper, purple for the orange giftwrap and turquoise for the blue giftwrap. But any colour scheme of your choice could be used, such as metallic gold or silver paper with red bows. This card is a great way of using up leftover pieces of giftwrapping paper and those odd lengths of quilling paper.

# IT'S A WRAP

Christmas cards can be fun, innovative and tell a tale, as here where a gift is surrounded by rolls of paper and ribbon as if in a frenzy of wrapping. The present is made in the same way as for the main card and glued to a purple card blank. Tiny pieces of tissue paper are glued to the card along with rolls of coloured papers to resemble wrapping paper, created by rolling small rectangles of paper around a cocktail stick (toothpick) and then gluing the end and removing the cocktail stick. For the ribbon, strips of coordinating papers are rolled around a needle tool and glued to the card.

# Swirly Trees

A quilled design that is simplicity itself can be as distinctive and elegant as the most complicated scheme. Here, three stylized coiled trees stand proudly in a row on a delicate tissue background. The motifs are made using wider paper to give them more prominence. The colour scheme of green and blue is contemporary and would be suitable for a male recipient.

**You will need . . . .**

- papers: 5mm (3/16in) wide turquoise, green
- card: cream, blue, green
- white fine tissue paper
- blue card blank

1 For the trunk of each tree, cut 6cm (2 3/8in) lengths of paper, two of turquoise and one of green. Then cut the following lengths of turquoise or green paper, to match the trunk, and glue to either side of the trunk, the longest attached first: 8cm (3 1/8in), 7cm (2 3/4in), 6cm (2 3/8in), 5cm (2in), 4cm (1 1/2in) lengths either side.

2 Using a needle tool, coil each length of paper attached to the trunk to the top. Start with the shortest length of paper and work along each of the lengths. Don't worry if the coils are tight, as they can be pulled looser to achieve the desired shape.

3 Put glue under the top of the trunk and a little on the coils – use a small amount only, or it will soak into the tissue paper. Position the green tree in the centre and a turquoise tree at an equal distance either side.

**SENTIMENTS SUGGESTIONS**

Have a Groovy Christmas!

Peace on Earth

Have Yourself a Jolly Holiday

May Your Christmas be Magical

**Tip . . .**

Each tree is surprisingly quick to create, making this project ideal for a beginner in quilling or for mass production.

## Tissue Tree

To save time, a single coiled tree is the main feature of this stylish design. The green tree, made as for the main card, is mounted onto a cream card square, then a larger blue card square, both with rounded corners, with a layer of tissue in between. A length of tissue is then added across the base of the tree. The tree panel is glued directly to a turquoise card blank with rounded corners to match. The design could easily be made into a tag by threading the tree panel with ribbon instead of gluing it to the card. Gemstones could be added to the ends of the coils, as in Crystal Snowflake, pages 32–33.

Tip . . .

The colour scheme of this card could be changed to something bolder and more unconventional, such as pinks and bright greens or even black and white.

# Finishing the Card

Cover a rectangle of cream card with fine white tissue paper and then mount onto blue card, then green card and finally a blue card blank. It's easy to make your own card blanks rather than using pre-cut and scored shop-bought blanks, but it's essential to use strong card, about 250gsm in weight. This is not only so that it will remain standing upright but can hold the weight of the decoration and motifs.

# Tall Tree Trio

Three swirly trees are individually framed and arranged vertically to make a tall narrow card. The swirly trees are made from 3mm (1/8in) wide paper in two colours, the top and bottom trees green and the middle tree blue. Each tree is mounted onto a cream square with rounded corners and then mounted onto slightly larger, round-cornered green squares. A strip of tissue paper is attached to a tall turquoise card and then the squares glued directly on top of the tissue. Alternatively, the middle tree could be omitted and a greeting added in its place on the cream card.

# Scrolled Noel

There are many types of font available for computers, so why not use one as inspiration for a decorative quilled script? In this sophisticated design, pinched coils are combined with open coils to create capital letters that spell out the traditional 'Noel' greeting in a unique way. Making a variety of letters in quilling need not be a daunting prospect, as they come together easily once you have created the basic shapes.

**You will need . . . .**

- paper: 2mm (1/16in) wide green
- card: light and dark green
- dark green long card blank

1 Begin by making loose closed coils from 10cm (4in) lengths of the green paper. Pinch several coils at either end to form leaf shapes. Take a 10cm (4in) length of the green paper and fold in half. Put glue in the centre fold and then gently press a leaf shape onto the glue so that the point of the shape fits into the fold. Wrap the paper length around the leaf.

2 This leaves two 'tails' around a pinched coil. Using a needle tool, coil the end of one of the 'tails' away from the centre, down to the leaf shape. Coil the other 'tail' in the same way. Repeat to make more of these shapes.

**Tip . . .**

Use other words to create alternative designs in different colour schemes, such as 'love' using reds or 'snow' using blues.

3 Position two shapes on a wide strip of light green card as shown, point to point. Then add another shape to the top to form part of the diagonal of the 'N'. Use a single leaf without tails for the centre of the diagonal and then another shape with tails to form the end of the diagonal.

## Short and Sweet

For a quicker card, choose a word with fewer letters as here. The 'J' is formed from two leaf shapes with tails glued point to point and coiled ends for the top of the letter, then a 10cm (4in) length coiled at the end for the hook, all glued to a wide strip of light green card. The 'O' is made as for the main card. For the 'Y', the down stroke is created from two leaf shapes with tails pointing towards each other with a non-tailed leaf shape in between. Then two leaf shapes with tails are glued pointing downwards to complete the letter. The light green card is mounted onto red card and then a dark green card blank with the fold at the top.

**Tip . . .**

This form of fancy script suits capital letters rather than lower case ones because of the structure of the shapes, but for an example of quilled lower case letters, see Festive Fonts, pages 34–35.

## Finishing the Card

Continue to build up the letters with a combination of shapes, as follows: N= six coils with tails and one leaf shape on its own; O= each side is a 10cm (4in) length with open coils; E= five coils; L = three coils. As with the Festive Fonts design on pages 34–35, it's best to glue both end letters in place first and work inwards, or to make light pencil marks where the letters will go. Mount the light green panel onto a slightly larger piece of dark green card and then onto a dark green long card blank with the fold at the top.

## Seasonal Sentiments

'Peace' is a word often used at Christmas, as it is a time to reflect and look forward to the New Year. Two pinched coils with tails are glued vertically to create the 'P', with a 10cm (4in) length of paper used to form the loop. The two 'E's are made as for the main card. The 'A' is formed from five coils with tails plus two single pinched coils in total, each 'leg' consisting of two coils with tails pointing outwards, with a single pinched coil in between. The remaining coil with tail is placed horizontally. The 'C' is two 10cm (4in) lengths coiled and glued next to each other. The letters are attached to a strip of cream card, which is mounted onto a wider strip of gold card, then green card. Finally, the lettering panel is mounted onto a gold card blank with the fold at the top.

# Gilded Garlands

Christmas is an ideal opportunity to indulge in the showiest, shiniest materials available to make stunning cards. Here, a light-catching pearlescent copper card blank provides the perfect background for flowing garlands of leaves studded with rich brown berries. The gold-edged paper used for the leaves adds to the luxurious effect, while the transfer letting brings a professional finish to the greeting.

## You will need . . . .

- papers: 3mm (1/8in) wide gold-edged ivory, brown
- card: brown, ivory
- pearlescent copper card blank
- transfer lettering or black pen

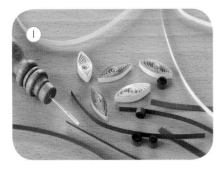

1 For the leaves, use 20cm (8in) lengths of the gold-edged ivory paper and a quilling tool to make loose closed coils – I have used 27 here. Pinch both ends of each coil to form teardrop shapes. Don't worry if they are different sizes – they shouldn't be uniform in any case. For the berries, form loose closed coils with 7cm (2 3/4in) lengths of the brown paper.

2 Attach a strip of brown card across the centre of the copper card blank, then mount the ivory card with the greeting on top. Glue the first coil of one garland to the copper card. Put a dot of glue on the tip of the coil and place a strip of the gold-edged ivory paper 18cm (7in) in length against the glue, to create the garland stem.

3 Place glue on one side of a berry and glue this onto the opposite side of the leaf, to keep the garland stem in place – in this way, you don't need to add glue to the edge of the length of paper at all. Continue to glue the leaves and berries in place all along the garland stem. You may need to trim the excess paper from the garland if it overhangs the edge of the card. Repeat for the second garland below the message.

## Tip . . .

If you don't have metallic-edged papers, a light covering of gold glitter glue would make the leaves sparkle.

## Burnished Branches

For an alternative festive leaf design, a square of cream card is mounted onto a square copper card blank. The leaves are made with 3mm (1/8in) wide copper-edged brown paper, again using 20cm (8in) lengths pinched at both ends. The berries are 7cm (2 3/4in) lengths of 3mm (1/8in) brown paper made into loose closed coils. The leaves, berries and branches are glued to the cream card in the same way as for the main card, then a small yellow gemstone attached to each corner. Finally, 'Seasons Greetings' is added with transfer lettering in gold on a strip of cream card, mounted with foam pads.

# FINISHING THE CARD

The card I have used here has the fold at the top, but the design works equally well if the fold is at the side. It's best to attach the brown card and cream card with the greeting on before positioning the coils, as it gives a boundary to work within. Also, it's more difficult to attach the strips of card after the coils have been glued on. I have used 27 leaves and 10 berries here, but you can add more or less as you wish. The colour schemes can also be changed to green leaves on a red background for a traditional scheme, or try black leaves on a white background for a dramatic modern effect. The message can alternatively be handwritten using calligraphy or produced on a computer.

# FALLING LEAVES

Branches cascade down vertically here to make a classic invitation, possibly for an evening party at Christmas. The leaves are made from 20cm (8in) lengths of 3mm (1/8in) cream paper, but this time without a gilded edge. The berries are 7cm (2 3/4in) lengths of 3mm (1/8in) copper-edged brown paper made into tight coils. The leaves, berries and branches are glued to a rectangle of brown card and then mounted onto a copper card blank. 'Invitation' is added using transfer lettering, but any greeting of your choice could be used instead.

# Hats & Mittens

Santa hats are a favourite festive symbol of the season and here two featuring fringed paper for the bobble and trim are juxtaposed with mittens on squares of contrasting card to form a grid pattern. The red and white colour scheme is in keeping with tradition, but with the motifs set against a pink and lime green background, it makes the design funky and fun. The cute mittens are made from just three simple quilled shapes glued together.

You will need . . . .

- papers: 10mm (3/8in) wide white; 3mm (1/8in) wide red, deep pink
- card: pink, lime green, red
- round-cornered red card blank
- 90-degree angle fringing tool
- corner rounder punch (optional)

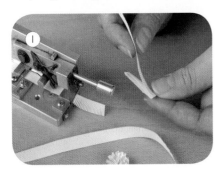

1 Fringe a long length of the white paper using the fringing tool. To make a bobble, insert a 15cm (6in) length of the fringed paper into a quilling tool and make a tight coil. Remove the tool, glue the end of the paper in place and then splay out the fringed ends. Make a second bobble in the same way. For the hat trim, fold over a 15cm (6in) fringed length several times and glue the end.

2 To make a hat, take a 20cm (8in) length of the red paper and make a loose closed coil with the quilling tool. Pinch one end tightly to a point and then use your fingers to pinch the other ends less tightly to make a triangle. Make a second hat in the same way. Round the corners of two squares of pink card and lime green card, using a corner rounder punch or scissors, and glue the hats to the pink squares. Glue the bobble and trim to each hat.

3 For the hand part of each mitten, make a 30cm (12in) length of the deep pink paper into a loose closed coil and pinch to create a flat base. For the thumb, repeat with a 15cm (6in) length of the same paper. For the mitten, make a 15cm (6in) length of the red paper into another loose closed coil and squeeze into a lozenge shape. Glue the three coils together to form the mitten on one of the rounded squares of lime green card, gluing on a second mitten facing the other way. Repeat for the second square of lime green card.

## Mitten Madness

For this bright card, a border of mittens surrounds a single bobble hat. The red hat with white fringed trim is made as for the main card and mounted onto a small square of green card, which is in turn mounted onto a larger rectangle of pink card, both with rounded corners. Twelve mittens are made as for main design, six of each colour, then glued directly to the pink card around the hat, alternating the colours. The pink card is glued to a wide strip of green card mounted onto a deeper pink, round-cornered card blank. A length of ribbon is tied around the spine of the card in a knot to finish.

**Tip . . .**

If you don't have a fringing tool, you can use a pair of fine-tipped scissors to fringe the paper.

## FINISHING THE CARD

Round the corners of a large square of red card, again either with the corner rounder punch or using scissors, and mount the pink and lime green panels onto it. Then mount this onto a larger square of pink card with rounded corners and in turn onto a round-cornered red card blank. The colour scheme of this card could be easily changed to blues and greens if the recipient is a boy (see Swirly Trees, pages 48–49).

## SNOW DRESSING

Blue and white snowflake patterned paper is the background for a sole Santa hat and a pair of mittens in this quick-to-make design. The snowflake paper is mounted onto a red card blank, both with matching rounded corners. A mini tag shape to display the mittens is cut from pink card, a hole made in the top and blue ribbon threaded through, which is then tied in a knot. This is mounted with foam pads onto the snowflake paper. The hat is glued to a round-cornered square of pink card, then also mounted with foam pads. A greeting such as 'Winter Wishes' or 'Christmas Sparkles' could be added to the card.

# SMILING SNOWMEN

This trio of quirky snowmen is a jolly way to welcome in the festive season. Double layers of white coils are used for the two shorter outer snowmen to make them fatter and fuller, while the tall, skinny central snowman is created from a stack of four white coils in a single layer. Patterned paper scarves, card hats and quilled buttons, eyes and noses add to the character of the figures, along with waving paper twig arms for a fun effect.

You will need.....

- paper: 3mm (1/8in) wide white, light and dark brown, orange; 2mm (1/16in) wide black
- blue card blank
- card: black, blue
- blue patterned paper

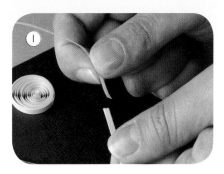

1 Tear lengths of the white paper, join together end to end to form a 120cm (4ft) length and use to make a loose closed coil with a quilling tool. Glue to the centre bottom of a blue card blank. Make another two coils in the same way and glue above the first. For the head, use an 80cm (32in) length of the white paper made into a loose closed coil. For the two snowmen either side, make loosed closed coils using a 160cm (63in) length of the white paper for the body and a 120cm (4ft) length for the head in the first layer, and a 120cm (4ft) length for the body and an 80cm (32in) length for the head in the second layer.

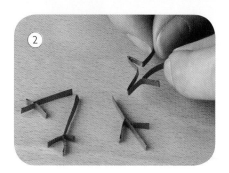

2 For the arms, take a 15cm (6in) length of the light or dark brown paper and apply glue to one side. Form into three loops and crease, then pressed the glued sides together as shown. Trim the excess paper. Make two arms from light brown and four from dark brown paper, then glue next to the snowmen.

3 For the noses, make loose closed coils from 20cm (8in) lengths of the orange paper and pinch into triangles (see page 12). Make tight coils from the black paper, as follows: eyes – 7cm (2 3/4in) lengths; buttons – 15cm (6in) lengths; mouths – 2cm (3/4in) lengths. Cut two hats from black card using the template on page 59.

Tip . . .

The colour scheme could be adapted to pinks and reds for a young girl or pastel blues for a baby's first Christmas.

## CUDDLY SNOWMAN

A little snowman looks cute on a bright-coloured card and is ideal to send to children or adapt into a tag. Here, the orange card frame against a bright green card blank echoes the snowman's orange nose and his green scarf. Two layers of white coils are mounted onto dark blue card using the instructions for the main card. The eyes, mouth, buttons and nose are then added, as well as a black hat cut out using the template on page 59. The scarf is cut from green paper with white spots and glued in place. Time is saved by not having to add arms to the snowman. A wavy strip of blue card is mounted across the bottom of the snowman using foam pads and the blue card mounted onto orange card and then a green card blank.

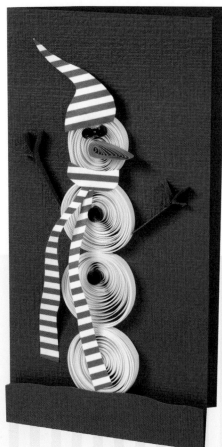

Tip . . .

These snowmen require long lengths of paper to be coiled, which can be a little challenging for a beginner to do.

# FINISHING THE CARD

Cut two scarf shapes from blue patterned paper and glue onto the two outer snowmen. Cut a wavy strip of blue card that matches the card blank and mount across the bottom of the snowmen using foam pads, to avoid the snowmen appearing to float in space. It's always a good idea to give motifs either a base or a horizon so that they don't hang in mid-air.

# TOWERING SNOWMAN

Making one tall snowman is a quicker alternative to the main design but without losing any of the impact. Here, four white quilled coils are glued in a column onto dark blue card, using the same measurements as those for the main card. The arms, nose, buttons and eyes are made following the main card instructions. A small piece of wavy blue card is mounted across the bottom coil using foam pads. For the snowman's hat, red and white striped paper is cut into a pointed hat shape and attached to the snowman's head. The same paper is cut into two long strands with a small piece cut for the neck, to make the scarf. This colour scheme could be adapted to fit the sporting colours of the recipient, such as their favourite football team colours.

# TEMPLATES

## TEXTURED TREE
Page 20

## FUNKY TREE
Pages 26–27

## PEAR TREE
Pages 22–23

## BOUNTIFUL BRANCHES
Page 22

# Pretty Patterns
Pages 20–21

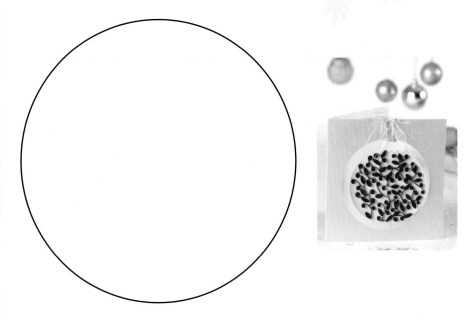

## Smiling Snowmen
Pages 56–57

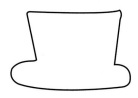

## Triangle Tree
Page 23

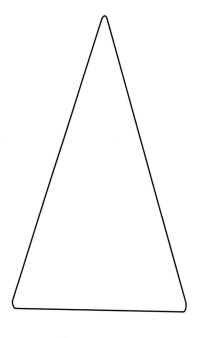

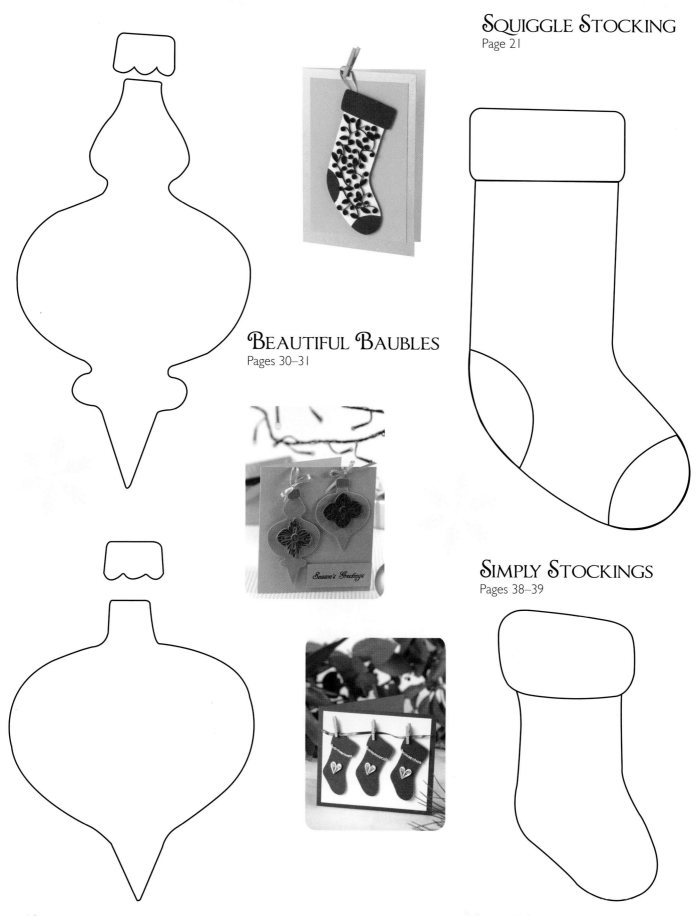

# BEAUTIFUL BAUBLES
Pages 30–31

# SIMPLY STOCKINGS
Pages 38–39

# Husking Template and Technique

Pages 30–31

The Beautiful Baubles design on pages 30–31 and variation cards use the technique of husking, where paper strips are wrapped around an arrangement of pins. If you are familiar with this technique, you simply need to copy the template in Step 1 below for the positions of the pins and then refer back to page 30 for the instructions. Beginners to this technique are taken here through the sequence of making the husking shape broken down into eight easy steps. The blue line represents the strip of paper and the black dots where the pins are inserted. Don't insert the pins all at once but one at a time, as illustrated in the photographic steps at the bottom of the page.

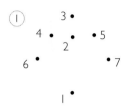
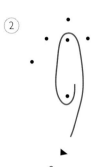

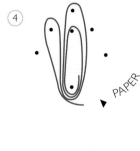

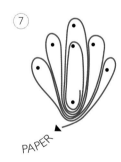
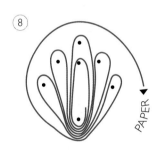

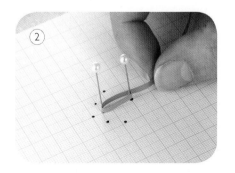
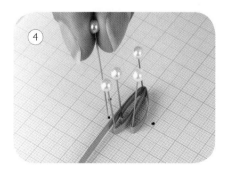
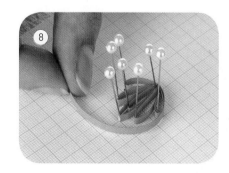

# SUPPLIERS

## UK

**Elderberry Crafts**
17 Elderberry Drive
Dereham
Norfolk
NR20 3ST
www.elderberrycrafts.com

**Jane Jenkins**
33 Mill Rise
Skidby
Cottingham
East Yorkshire
HU16 5UA
www.jjquilling.co.uk

**Katy Sue Designs**
Henry Robson Way
South Shields
Tyne and Wear
NE33 1RF
www.flower-soft.co.uk
For Flower Soft® products used in
Festive Fonts, pages 34–35

**Letraset Ltd**
Wotton Road
Ashford
Kent
TN23 6FL
www.letraset.com

## USA

**Lake City Craft Company**
1209 Eaglecrest Street
PO Box 2009
Nixa, Missouri 65714
www.quilling.com

**Swarovski**
See www.swarovski-crystallized.
com for local stockists of the
crystals used in Crystal Snowflake,
pages 32–33

## AUSTRALIA

**Jonathan Mayne**
PO Box 345
Mt Martha
VIC 3934
www.jonathanmayne.com.au

## USEFUL WEBSITES

**Dutch Quilling Guild**
www.filigraan.nl

**North American Quilling Guild**
(NAQG)
www.naqg.org

**UK Quilling Guild**
www.quilling-guild.co.uk

## ABOUT THE AUTHOR

Elizabeth Moad is a busy papercrafter, workshop tutor and author. Elizabeth is accomplished in many crafting techniques, but is widely known for her talent in quilling. She is a regular contributor to UK magazines *Crafts Beautiful* and *Let's Make Cards!* This is Elizabeth's fifth book and her work has been featured in several other card-making books.

Books published by David & Charles, by Elizabeth Moad: *Thrilling Quilling, Cards for Lads and Dads, Quick and Clever Christmas Cards* and *The Papercrafter's Bible.*

## ACKNOWLEDGEMENTS

Many thanks to the team of friends who worked on my book, and made it all possible. Karl Adamson provided the professional photography and creative styling. Jo Richardson edited my words with her usual panache and flair. And a big thank you to Sarah Wade of Design House Studios (www.designhousestudios.co.uk) who worked tirelessly on the layout of this book to create its fabulous look.

# INDEX